The Little Book
of Team Games

by Simon MacDonald
Illustrations by Marion Lindsay

LITTLE BOOKS WITH BIG IDEAS

Featherstone Education
An imprint of Bloomsbury Publishing Plc

50 Bedford Square
London
WC1B 3DP
UK

1385 Broadway
New York
NY 10018
USA

www.bloomsbury.com

Bloomsbury is a registered trademark of Bloomsbury Publishing Plc

First published 2015

Text © Simon MacDonald, 2015
Illustrations © Marion Lindsay, 2015
Cover photographs © LEYF/Shutterstock, 2015

British Library Cataloguing-in-Publication Data
A catalogue record for this book is available from the British Library.

ISBN:
PB 978-1-4729-1682-2
ePDF 978-1-4729-1683-9

Library of Congress Cataloging-in-Publication Data
A catalog record for this book is available from the Library of Congress.

1 3 5 7 9 10 8 6 4 2

Printed and bound in India by Replika Press Pvt. Ltd.

This book is produced using paper that is made from wood grown in managed, sustainable forests. It is natural, renewable and recyclable. The logging and manufacturing processes conform to the environmental regulations of the country of origin.

To view more of our titles please visit
www.bloomsbury.com

Contents

Introduction

There is an interesting and emotive debate concerning the 'winning and losing' aspect of competitive games. Most people would accept that there is a competitive edge to games and sports that has to be acknowledged. This can result in some children feeling discouraged from playing games, and a drop in self-esteem and unwillingness to participate in such activities in the future can have potentially catastrophic results as the child progresses through their education. This must be avoided at all costs.

A hugely beneficial aspect of involvement in games is that children can measure their new best effort against their previous achievement, and at the same time strive to improve their skills. It is also true that for some children, sporting competition is one area of their education in which they excel, and rather than deny them this we must work to find a way to strike a happy medium between the two extremes.

This book aims to do just that. By drawing on the experience of over twenty years in teaching, I hope to be able to offer a means by which competition (within reason) and teamwork can be promoted in a healthy, enjoyable and productive way. I reference 'old school' games, many of which I remember from my own childhood and have subsequently adapted for use here, as well as including regional variations of games in order to celebrate the diversity and richness of team game-playing across the UK and beyond.

Let the games commence...

Simon MacDonald

Links with the Early Learning Goals

The playing of games teaches us many of the social skills necessary for a balanced, healthy and productive lifestyle. Through games we learn how to share, take turns and celebrate our own successes, as well as learning how to commiserate with each other and applaud the efforts of our opponents, friends and peers. Games play a fantastic role in the development of concentration and attention, self-esteem and group work, and rules provide the framework for us to assimilate the moral values expected of us as members of society – games and game-playing should not be underestimated. Games underpin the entire teaching and learning process, and this lasts a lifetime.

The following Early Learning Goals are particularly relevant to game playing in the following ways:

Prime areas
Communication and language
▶ Interact with others and take turns
▶ Sustain attentive listening, responding to what they have heard by relevant comments, questions or actions
▶ Speak clearly and audibly, with confidence
▶ Use language to imagine and recreate roles and experiences

Physical development
▶ Move safely with confidence and imagination
▶ Move with control and co-ordination
▶ Show awareness of their own space and that of others

Personal, social and emotional development
▶ Continue to be interested, excited and motivated to learn
▶ Maintain attention, concentration and sit quietly when appropriate
▶ Form good relationships with adults and peers
▶ Work as part of a group, taking turns and sharing fairly, understanding that there needs to be agreed values and codes of behaviour

Specific areas
Expressive arts and design
▶ Use their imagination in creative activities
▶ Express and communicate their ideas, thoughts and feelings

Why play team games?

There is an interesting and emotive debate concerning the 'winning' and 'losing' aspects of competitive team games. Most of us will accept that there is a necessarily competitive edge to all games and sports and this must be acknowledged. What is beneficial is the fact that children can learn to win and lose in a supportive environment while measuring their previous achievements against new best efforts, as well as continually striving to improve their group skills.

It is important that all children taking part in these games are allowed the freedom to show their support for their team and also learn about 'sporting' behaviour. Some will find winning and losing difficult. Others may get annoyed with the efforts of others. What is essential is that each example of this is an opportunity for teaching and learning. There is nothing wrong with promoting competitiveness in games, but there is an awful lot to be criticised regarding a 'win at all costs' mentality.

This book contains over 30 team games that (with the exception of one or two, as noted) can be played either indoors or out, together with variations and advice for carrying them out. Every one can be used with groups of all ages and each can be adapted to suit varying abilities, the confidence of facilitator and target group as well as size of setting.

Tips for sorting children into teams

Teams of two

When promoting team games in an Early Years setting, it is essential to first create a safe and supportive environment for playing and, as a direct consequence, for learning to take place. There are a huge number of ways in which you can organise children into groups or teams – you are simply limited by your own imagination – so the following list is by no means exhaustive. I have used these strategies and found them to be very useful in avoiding anxiety or that horrible sense of being left out. Of course, not every suggestion will be appropriate for every group or circumstance, but you know your groups better than anyone so go with what seems best.

- ▶ **Apples or bananas?:** This simple choice of food preference as a way of making teams can be adapted to include all sorts of other favourites: colours, animals, TV programmes, etc.
- ▶ **Nail freeze:** Give the instruction "Look at your nails and FREEZE!" Those with their palms up are in one team and those their palms turned down are in the other.

- ▶ **Thumbs up:** Give the instruction "Clasp your hands!" Those with their right thumb on top will be in one team and those with their left thumb on top will be in the other.
- ▶ **Hands up:** Following this self-explanatory instruction, those with their left hand up are in one team and those with their right raised are in another.
- ▶ **Even numbers:** Ask the children to count how many letters make up their first name – help those who struggle with this. Those with an even number make up one team and those with an odd number make another.
- ▶ **Close one eye:** Those with the left eye closed are in one team and those with the right eye closed form the other.
- ▶ **Fingers or thumbs?:** Ask the children to put either a finger or thumb in the air and waggle it about. Then direct them to join the other children who did the same as them.
- ▶ **Holidays:** Give the children the option of a holiday in the sun or in the snow to make two teams.
- ▶ **Shoes:** Divide the children into two groups – those with laces and those without – or those with laces and those with velcro.
- ▶ **Tongue twisters:** Ask the children whether they can curl their tongues. Those that can make one team and those that can't (or would prefer not to!) make another.
- ▶ **Brothers and sisters:** There are a number of variables here. You could ask for those who have three siblings or more to be in one team and those with two or fewer to be in another.
- ▶ **Do you feel like...?:** Ask the children if they feel like one thing or another – these can be obscure as you like. For example, "Do you feel like a tennis racquet or a tennis ball?" Divide the teams by whichever they choose.

The next selection carries a word of caution. All of the above, and – it is hoped – those below, are excellent team-formers as well as being fun, interesting and a terrific opportunity for children to share information with everyone. However, as we consider the fact that we are dealing with the subject of teamwork and competition, the last thing we want is to draw attention to certain differences that may be seen as favouring the 'haves' against the 'have-nots'. This could soon become an undesirable 'better' or 'worse' judgment that the children are being led to make and that must be guarded against. Therefore, it might be simpler, fairer and kinder to state "Those who saw shooting stars in the summer join up in a group over here," rather than say "Those who saw shooting stars in the summer join up over here and those who didn't join together here."

- ▶ Join up if you would like to play a musical instrument
- ▶ Join up if you have been to a wedding
- ▶ Join up if you like to use a computer
- ▶ Join up if you can swim
- ▶ Join up if you can climb
- ▶ Join up if you like to ride a bike/trike
- ▶ Join up if you like running
- ▶ Join up if you saw dolphins in the summer
- ▶ Join up if you like barbecues
- ▶ Join up if you know someone who is a doctor or a nurse. (Or a dentist or a teacher. Or a fire-fighter or a paramedic. Or a soldier or a sailor. Or a pilot or a vet or any other job that you can think of!)

Finally, here is a fantastic and fun way of choosing two sides that appears to have many names and variations. I know it as 'Ducks and Cows' but I have seen and heard it called many other combinations of animals that span the A to Z! Just one word of warning – with the best will in the world, it is the lot of the Early Years educator to sometimes appear insensitive with the children in their care and in this game it is wise to avoid any animal or animal combination that may infer a stigma – elephants as large, monkeys as naughty, pigs as dirty, etc. – keep it simple and non-contentious!

- ▶ You can form a circle if you wish but it is not necessary, as you will see. Ask everyone to close their eyes – this may be difficult for some children, so encourage them to try and if unwilling or anxious, say that they can look down at the floor and/or cover their eyes with their hand. The judicious placing of a member of staff next to this participant will usually allay any concerns. You or any other 'leader' then moves around the space and whispers either 'duck' or 'cow' in their ears. As the last child receives their instruction, but still with their eyes closed, all the ducks start quacking and all the cows start mooing. They then move slowly around the space, with their eyes closed, and try to find other 'cows' or 'ducks' to form their teams. It is all really rather silly but very good fun. You as leader should try to keep out of the way and act as 'spotter' while this activity takes place – the children need to be safe at all times, which means no collisions!

Teams of three or more

My last thought on ways to divide groups involves making more than two teams, as sometimes numbers demand it. Here are a few more suggestions. Depending on the ages and abilities of the children, more support from staff/adult helpers (or even older children, if you work in a larger setting) may be required and/or useful with some of these activities.

▶ Everyone says/sings/shouts the first vowel of their name. Once the A's, E's, I's, O's and U's are gathered in their teams there will be five groups that can be adjusted to equal numbers ready for a team game.

▶ Ask everyone to hold up any number of fingers between one and five. Without any talking (I know!), have the children get together with others who held up the same number of fingers.

▶ Get into teams of any number according to colour of clothing.

▶ Get into teams of any number with others who were born in the same season/month/day.

▶ As a starter activity, get into teams of three (with the two children next to them) and make the letter shape 'N' – although any letter with the same component lines will do – or smaller/bigger numbers with letters that have more or less component lines. You could also ask for lower case letters, and sometimes this is easier as cursive shapes tend to blend their component lines.

▶ The same could be done with numbers – for both of these activities it is a good idea to have the numbers and letters drawn large on cards, or the resources to display them clearly such as a white/smartboard. This has the added benefit of the children being shown letter and numeral formation – win-win!

Of course, you know your children best and each of your settings will have group and sub-group organisational systems that work effectively for you. I have found that with each new activity that has come my way, I have managed to adapt and adopt at will – I'm sure that the same is true of you.

Balloon-a-ball

This game has a fun party feel to it, and is an excellent way of helping children improve their hand-eye co-ordination.

Group size:

Any

Equipment:

▶ A volleyball, badminton or tennis net (or suitable alternative), raised higher or lower to make the game easier or more difficult

▶ Balloons – and lots of them!

I will need

How to play:

1. This is an indoor game and on no account should it be attempted outside – even if it appears to be a beautiful, calm, windless summer day!

2. By using one of the team-making activities listed on page 6, form two teams of children and have them stand on either side of the net. You could begin by simply laying the net in a line across the floor.

3. The game begins by you introducing a blown up balloon – the 'balloon-a-ball' – to each team, and then directing the children to hit it, volleyball-style, across the net (or over the line). The balloon will travel so slowly that the children will have more than enough time to track and then hit the balloon-a-ball before it touches the ground.

Variations/advice:

▶ Add the instruction to catch the balloon-a-ball for extra points.

▶ Introduce further balloons – this has the benefit of involving more of the children so no-one is left standing still for long. It builds confidence as the success ratio is high and, even if a balloon is grounded, you and they do not spend most of the session chasing balloons around the space.

▶ Use a simple scoring system for each balloon that hits the ground, and/or for each time the balloon crosses the net/line.

▶ Warn the children that balloons burst and they make a loud bang – reassure them that it is OK to feel a little frightened. I also suggest that you spend a little more money on good quality latex balloons as this mitigates the risk. You could even try using an 'extra-points' rule if the balloon does burst, rather than making it a negative experience... don't mention this at the beginning of the game though, as it is asking for trouble!

The runaway train

This is a very good game for encouraging teamwork and synchronised movement. It works best when played in a large open space.

Group size:

Any

Equipment:

▶ Soft-play equipment/PE apparatus

How to play:

1. Beforehand, set out a defined circuit/'track' in an open space in your setting, that will eventually lead them back to the start.

2. Choose a two-team sorting activity from page 6, and then get the two teams of children to line up, each child facing forward, with the two lines standing parallel to each other. Direct them to place their hands on the waist of the child in front of them, one hand on the shoulder, or any other safe way of linking. The child at the front of each line is the 'engine'.

3. Starting at the 'station', both trains weave around the defined space, and all the children sing continuously the verse below from 'The runaway train went over the hill'. At the end of each verse, the child at the back comes to the front to be the engine and takes his/her turn leading the train.

> *The runaway train went over the hill and she blew, she blew.*
> *The runaway train went over the hill and she blew, she blew.*
> *The runaway train went over the hill, the last I heard she was blowing still,*
> *And she blew, blew, blew, blew, blew.*

4. The winner is the train that gets back to the station first!

Variations/advice:

▶ Try adding some obstacles and gradients to the track. If you are confident in the ability of the children to move safely in a more challenging test, perhaps set out some parallel, low balance beams as rails and move along this track.

▶ The train could be driven at different speeds and the children could use different movements.

▶ You may want to add goods to the train – the last truck could drag a blanket carrying soft toys behind it, for instance. If so, remember that the switching of places at the end of each verse is probably best avoided! Alternatively, each train could be a 'shunting engine' and push a box or crate of toys in front – care is needed in the selection of materials and this will depend on the surface environment.

▶ Ribbons or lengths of crêpe paper on sticks, one in each hand, can be used to make the circular movements of the wheels. Moving about the space in this way works as a visually-pleasing spectacle and an alternative to the children holding on to each other.

Kick the can

This game, also known a 'Kick the cone', is a variation of 'Tag' and 'Hide and Seek'.

Group size:

Equal numbers, in two teams (5-12 children per team)

Equipment:

▶ A soft-play shape or plastic cone

How to play:

1. Place a can or cone in the middle of the area.

2. One team of players is 'It'; the other team runs off and hides, while the 'It' team cover their eyes and count to an agreed number.

3. Children in the 'It' team then try to find members of the opposite team.

4. If a player is tagged by 'It', they go into a holding pen for captured players, or alternatively they can join 'It' in trying to capture the other team.

5. If one of the 'free' players manages to reach the middle and kick the can or cone without being captured by 'It', the captured players and those who have changed sides are released.

6. The game is over once the 'It' team players have captured all of the other players.

Variations/advice:

▶ Having two adults working with each team can encourage communication and strategy if the children are struggling.

▶ The team trying to kick the can could be asked before the game begins for ways in which they could try to do this, while the 'It' team could be asked to suggest ways of defending the can.

Snake in the alley

This game, also known as 'Snake in the gutter', tests children's agility and strategy.

Group size:

10+

Equipment:

▶ Chalk to draw team lines

16

How to play:

1. At least four players are the snakes.

2. The snakes form the alley by standing in a line with wide spaces between them, facing the rest of the group, who should be at a distance.

3. The adult in charge (or a child) yells 'Snake in the alley!', and the children try to weave through the alley without being tagged (touched by a hand on the body) by a snake.

4. Those who get tagged are now snakes and stay in the alley to try to tag others in the next run. Those who make it through the alley without being tagged can make another run in the next round – but anyone who is tagged must join the snakes.

5. You can continue the game until everyone has been caught. If you want to play again, make sure that different children are chosen to start as snakes this time round.

Variations/advice:

▶ If a child is worried about making a run through the alley, they could be partnered with a more confident player.

▶ The alley could be enlarged to make it easier (the 'snakes' stand with wider gaps between them) and, as the game progresses, these gaps could shrink in size.

▶ The emphasis should be on the two opposing teams working with each other: one adult should support, encourage and advise the runners, while another should work with the snakes, suggesting strategies to tag the runners.

Red rover

This is a very good game for encouraging teamwork and synchronised movement.

Group size:

10+

Equipment:

▶ 8 or more lengths of ribbon (or scarves), each approximately 1 metre long

How to play:

1. Divide the children into two teams and choose a leader for each team.

2. The players should form two parallel lines opposite each other. The players in each line should stand about a metre apart, holding lengths of ribbon to connect the line.

3. The leader of one team chooses one player from the opposite team and invites them to play by calling 'Red rover, red rover, send (child's name) on over!'

4. The player called then runs at one of the lengths of ribbon held by the opposing team and tries to run through the ribbon and break the chain. If he/she fails, he/she joins that line and the turn passes to the other team.

5. The game ends when one team has all but one of the players in their line.

Variations/advice:

▶ At the end of the game, the lone player could decide on the new teams for a new game – it all depends on their (and your!) energy levels at this point!

Hunter and watcher

This activity gives the children experience in game-playing that not only includes teams but also offers up other roles within an imaginative scenario.

Group size:

10+

Equipment:

▶ None needed

How to play:

1. One player (someone quick and fast) is chosen to be the 'hunter', and another (more patient) player is chosen to be the 'watcher'. The rest of the children split into two teams, and each team decides on an animal that they are going to be.

2. Mark out a circle about 10 feet in diameter on the ground in the middle of the playing area, using chalk, stones, sticks or whatever else you think appropriate. The watcher stays in this 'pen' for the duration of the game, patrolling the perimeter and trying to catch any stray animals that come too close!

3. The animals scatter, and start to run around the play area, trying to escape the hunter. If the hunter catches an animal, he leads him over to the pen. Once in the pen you cannot escape, but you can be rescued on the way to the pen if one of the other animals touches you. However, your rescuer must avoid being touched by the hunter, or he too will be caught and put in the pen!

Variations/advice:

▶ You can stop the game at any time, but you might want to set a time limit in advance or declare an end when a certain number of animals have been caught.

▶ This is a great game if you have one child that doesn't like running around too much, as they can be actively involved in the guard position.

Red light, green light

This outdoor game is a variation on 'Grandmother's footsteps', and is suitable for children of all ages. You will need quite a bit of space! It is an excellent way of reinforcing the concept that 'red is for stop' and 'green is for go'.

Group size:

10+

Equipment:

▶ Chalk to draw starting line

How to play:

1. One player (or a practitioner) is chosen to be the caller. The caller stands facing away from the other children, who stand behind a starting line drawn up about 30 feet (10 metres) away.

2. When the caller calls out 'green light', the children run forward to try to tag him. They must move as quickly as possible, but at any time the caller may call out 'red light', at which point all the children must freeze, and the caller turns around. If he catches anyone moving – even a tiny bit! – they are sent back to the starting line.

3. The first player to tag the caller becomes caller in the next round.

Variations/advice:

▶ Introduce an 'amber light', where some movement is allowed if players are frozen in an awkward or difficult-to-balance stance!

Cat and mouse

This is a great game to play at any spare moment, and involves a fun chant.

Group size:

10+

Equipment:

▶ None needed

How to play:

1. One child is chosen to be the cat (the chaser) and one child is chosen to be the mouse. All the other children form a circle, holding hands, with the mouse inside and the cat outside.

2. The children in the circle move around while calling out the following rhyme:

   What time is it?

   Just struck nine.

   Is the cat at home?

   He's about to dine!

3. When the rhyme stops, the children forming the circle stop moving, and the mouse starts to weave in and out of the ring of children. The cat starts to chase the mouse, weaving in and out; he or she MUST follow the mouse's exact path.

4. When the cat catches the mouse, two more children can take a turn at being cat and mouse and the game continues.

Hopping chicken

Once the children have got the hang of this activity, it can be played as a race or relay to increase the element of competitiveness.

Group size:

10+

Equipment:

▶ 10 sticks (each about 12 inches long, blunted or soft-capped at each end)

How to play:

1. Each player (or pair) has five sticks that are laid on the ground about 10 inches apart.

2. One player from each team starts, hopping over the sticks without touching any of them. If a stick is touched, the player is disqualified.

3. When the player has hopped over all the sticks he stops, still on one foot, and bends down to pick up the last stick. He then hops back over the remaining sticks.

4. Reaching the beginning again, he drops the stick to one side and sets off again to hop over the nine remaining sticks, pick up the last one, and return. If playing in teams of two, the first player switches with the second player at this stage. Play continues until all of the sticks have been picked up.

5. Remember, a player is disqualified if they put both feet on the ground at any point during their turn, or if they touch a stick with their foot.

6. The winner is the player or team that has got the furthest along when all other players/teams are disqualified.

Variations/advice:

▶ Use a different scoring system, in which you count the mistakes: the winner is the team that finishes with the least mistakes.

▶ Play as a race game. If you make a mistake, you start over.

▶ Play as a relay. The first player hops over ten sticks, returning with the tenth. The second player hops over nine, the third hops over eight, etc.

▶ Try changing the foot that you hop on in each round.

Hawks and chicks

This traditional Filipino game encourages children to communicate well, develop strategies and work as a team, and will develop cooperation as well as agility.

Group size:

6+

Equipment:

▶ None needed

How to play:

1. One child is chosen to be the hawk, and another the hen. All the other children are chicks, and line up behind the hen, holding onto the waist of the child in front of them.

2. The hawk and the hen face each other, and the hawk tries to catch the chicks. The hen's goal is to protect her chicks, by holding out her hands and moving from side to side to block the hawk, with her chicks moving in a line behind her. When the hen moves, the chicks should also move in the same direction so it is difficult for the hawk to catch them.

3. Any chicks that are caught move over to stand behind the hawk and become part of the team trying to catch the chicks, and the line of chicks closes up. The last chick in line is usually the hardest to catch!

Variations/advice:

▶ Set a time limit and keep score.

▶ Remember to allow all players to be both the hawk and a chick – this is important in order to develop both dodging and chasing skills.

Where do you stand?

This simple game can also be used as a starter activity to divide the children into teams for further games.

Size of group:
10+

Equipment:
▶ Chalk

How to play:

1. Using chalk (or other means), mark out a line down the centre of your space. All the children start by standing on the line.

2. Now call out pairs of opposites, and point in one direction for each. Children make their choice and run to their chosen side of the line.

   Examples of opposites might be:

   ▶ Cats or dogs?

   ▶ Rabbits or mice?

   ▶ Football or rugby?

   ▶ Country or town?

   ▶ Hot dogs or hamburgers?

   ▶ Cereal or toast?

   ▶ Maths or English?

   ▶ Tinkerbell or Peter Pan?

   Try to also think up some opposites that will get all of the children on one side of the line!

Variations/advice:

▶ If you are playing indoors and you want the children to get a little more exercise, you can tell them to sit down once they have run over to their chosen side – they'll soon be up and moving around again!

▶ Once you've assessed those who understand and are playing the game well, you could offer them the chance to be 'caller', where they come up with the pairs of opposites.

▶ Ask older children to run the game and get them to record how many players choose each side.

Line up

This game requires children to practise their numerical and observational skills, and also encourages discussion.

Group size:

5+ players per team

Equipment:

► None needed

How to play:

1. Separate everyone into teams as per one of the strategies on page 6: 5 or 6 children per team is ideal. Older children or other practitioners could act as facilitators and offer organisational help with the following directions.

2. One person is the caller. They call out 'Everyone please now line up... ' and complete the sentence with an instruction (see suggestions below).

3. All the players should try to sort themselves into the correct order in the quickest time possible, and shout when they are finished. Here are some ideas:

   ▶ By birthday: oldest first

   ▶ By first name: alphabetical order

   ▶ By height: shortest first

   ▶ According to how many cousins you have: least number of cousins first

   ▶ By colour of your top: rainbow order

   ▶ By colour of your top: alphabetical order

   ▶ By how much hair you have on your head: least hair first

Try to also think up some opposites that will get all the children on one side of the line!

Variations/advice:

▶ Once the children have got the hang of it, you could make some rounds – or the whole game – silent. In this instance, players can only communicate with gestures.

Throwing squares

This is a very simple game that allows children to practise their gross motor skills and co-ordination as well as their counting.

Group size:

10+

Equipment:

▶ Small soft throwing objects such as beanbags

▶ Chalk/masking tape (for an outdoor game); or

▶ Paper/felt (for an indoor game)

How to play:

1. Draw a rectangle – about 24 inches by 12 inches – on the ground using chalk or masking tape. Alternatively, cut one out of paper or felt for an indoor game. Divide the rectangle in two so that you have two squares side by side. Draw or mark a further line about 8 feet away from the long side of the rectangle (you can adjust the distance according to age and ability).

2. Sort the children into two teams. Each side will need a soft throwing object such as a small beanbag.

3. One player places his object in one of the two squares. The other player moves to stand behind the line and tries to throw his object to land in the same square as the other player's object.

4. The first team to reach the previously agreed score wins.

Score as follows:

▶ The same square: 2 points

▶ The other, empty square: 1 point

▶ Outside the target: 0 points

Variations/advice:

▶ Children could have fun designing their own portable felt version of this game to be played indoors. First make the board out of felt, and add decoration with marker pen as desired. Then make two flat felt beanbags in different colours. You could make a simple drawstring bag to keep the game in, too.

▶ For an outdoor game, the children could make up a set of two evenly-sized pebbles, painted or otherwise marked to distinguish them, and a piece of chalk.

▶ Divide the rectangle into thirds, or even quarters, to increase the level of difficulty.

Fill the basket

This game provides another fun way of developing both aim and numerical skills simultaneously.

Group size:

10+

Equipment:

▶ Chalk to draw a throwing line

▶ A variety of soft throwing objects: two of each item

▶ Two baskets, boxes or bins

How to play:

1. Collect pairs of as many different throwing objects as possible, such as balls, beanbags and soft toys.

2. Sort the children into two teams and explain that their aim is to fill their basket with the objects before the other team manages it.

3. Two children, one from each team, comes forward to the line to take their turn at selecting an object and trying to throw it into the basket. They must stay behind the line when they throw; crossing it incurs a penalty!

4. The team who fills their basket first wins.

Variations/advice:

▶ Give each different object a higher or lower point score. For instance, Frisbee could gain you 20 points if it lands in the basket, whereas a beanbag may only score 5 points.

▶ To make the game easier or harder, you could move the throwing line for each team closer or further away. You could also reduce or increase the size of the basket/recepticle.

Throwing fists

Practise counting and co-ordination with this game of predictions!

Group size:

5+ players per team

Equipment:

▶ None needed

How to play:

1. The children form two teams and line up facing each other.

2. On the count of three, the children in one team throw one fist in front of them, each with anything from nought to five fingers extended. At the same time, one child from the other team (take it in turns) does the same and calls out a number. The number should be his or her guess of the total number of fingers held up. If the total number of fingers extended add up to that number, the child wins.

3. Of course, the child must call out a number that might come up. So if five children are playing on each side, the numbers can be between nought and twenty-five; if three children are playing, between nought and fifteen, and so on.

4. Children must be careful to throw their fists out on time, too, so that no child can be accused of changing their fingers after the number is called!

Variations/advice:

▶ The children will soon learn that if they are displaying zero fingers themselves they should call low, and vice versa. You could use this game to teach about odd and even numbers.

▶ Try the variation 'Fingers out': The children form two teams and each faces the other, so that every child has an opponent. The children count to 3, and on '3' they put out one hand – either as a fist or with 1, 2 or 3 fingers extended, at the same time calling out a number between 1 and 6. For each pair, add up the number of fingers extended. If a child guessed the exact number of fingers shown, they score 2 points. If they guessed nearest the number of fingers shown, they score 1 point. If there is a tie, no points are scored. The first child in each pair who reaches (or exceeds) a given number or points (perhaps five or ten) wins.

A big wind blows

This game is a variation of 'Musical Chairs', and is a fun way of helping the children get to know each other.

Group size:

10+

Equipment:

▶ Chairs

▶ A large space

▶ Two sets of differently coloured bibs or sashes

How to play:

1. Arrange the chairs in a circle, facing the middle, and ask all the children to sit down. Give each child a coloured bib – alternate as you go round the circle. The two colours denote the two teams.

2. An adult stands outside the circle and calls out 'A big wind blows for everyone who....'. Fill in the blank with a statement that will affect some of the group from each team (see ideas below). Anyone who is affected must stand up and find another chair that is at least two chairs away from their own.

3. The practitioner should quickly remove one of the chairs from the circle as soon as the children stand up and begin moving. The child who cannot find a chair moves outside the circle and helps the adult to come up with ideas for the next 'big wind'. The winning team is the one with the last player left in the circle.

Ideas include:

- ▶ A big wind blows for everyone who has a little brother
- ▶ A big wind blows for everyone who has a big sister
- ▶ A big wind blows for everyone who has been to France
- ▶ A big wind blows for everyone who has a dog
- ▶ A big wind blows for everyone who ate cornflakes for breakfast this morning
- ▶ A big wind blows for everyone who likes... (insert a popular TV show, game or celebrity)

Variations/advice:

▶ It is wise to have enough adult helpers to remove chairs safely and also ensure that the players are as protected as possible.

▶ For a variation that does not have a winner and that allows children more involvement, all of the children sit on a chair except for one child who stands in the middle. The child standing in the middle calls out: 'A big wind blows for everyone who....', then fills in the blank with a statement that relates to his or herself. Anyone who shares the chosen characteristic must stand up, and the standing players (including the child in the middle) try to find an empty chair that is at least two chairs away from their own. The child who cannot get to an empty chair in time moves into the middle of the circle and comes up with the idea for the next 'big wind'. With this variation, all of the children stay in play until they have had enough!

Beanbag rush

This game will create a lively party atmosphere and is a straightforward but effective way of encouraging teamwork and co-operation.

Group size:

5+ players per team

Equipment:

▶ Small beanbags (one per team)

How to play:

1. Divide the children into teams and line them up in rows, one behind the other but with a little bit of space between each. Give the child at the front of each row a beanbag.

2. The children must now pass the beanbag from one child to the next and back again, in a particular style, which you can decide on as appropriate for the ages and abilities of the children in your setting.

Here are some 'passing' ideas to get you started:

▶ Up the row, right hand only

▶ Up the row, left hand only

▶ Down the row, both hands

▶ Up the row, right hand over left shoulder

▶ Down the row, left hand over right shoulder

▶ Up the row, under the right leg

▶ Down the row, under the left leg

Variations/advice:

▶ It might be a good idea to have a practice game first!

▶ If a beanbag is dropped, you can make the children start again from the beginning or from the front of the row.

▶ Race to find out who can pass all of the beanbags correctly, in the quickest time.

Otedama

Otedama is a traditional Japanese game, similar to Jacks, and is played with five small beanbags called 'ojami'. The ojami were often made using scraps of kimonos. To add another dimension to this activity, you could make your own ojami – otherwise, ready-made beanbags work just as well.

Group size:

10+ (ideally an even number – alternatively, one of the players can be chosen to take another turn)

Equipment:

▶ Five ojami (see on the next page) or small beanbags

How to play:

1. Sort the children into two teams and ask them to line up in two rows, one behind the other.

2. Scatter the five beanbags on the floor. Pick up one and toss it high into the air. With the same hand, while the first beanbag is in the air, pick up another and transfer it to your other hand. Then catch the thrown beanbag in the other.

3. Scatter the beanbags again. This time pick up two beanbags to transfer, and so on. If successful, repeat again, each time trying to transfer one more beanbag while the first one is still in the air, until you have four beanbags in one hand and catch the fifth in the other. Players will need to get progressively quicker!

4. Play moves to the next team member when a round is unsuccessful, and the unsuccessful player moves to the back of the line.

Variations/advice:

▶ Toss five beanbags into the air and catch as many as you can on the back of the same hand. Flip the bags that you caught into the air again and catch as many as you can in the palm of the same hand.

▶ For a slightly more difficult challenge, throw one beanbag up into the air – then, with the other hand, pick up a beanbag and wedge it between the fingers of the throwing hand, in time to catch the original beanbag. Throw again, and wedge another. Continue until four beanbags are wedged and the thrown beanbag is caught again!

Balloon pop!

This is an effective way of channeling children's excess energy into a game – you may want to play it outdoors!

Group size:

5+ players per team

Equipment:

▶ Chalk to draw team lines, or any other means to show the two sides

▶ Two large baskets or dustbin liners

▶ Lots of inflated balloons

How to play:

1. It is important to make sure that all participants are happy to join in before you begin this game. The popping/banging of balloons can be great fun for some, but others may find it scary and/or may be noise-sensitive – choose your participants carefully.

2. Divide the children into two equal groups and line them up.

3. A little distance away (you decide, as appropriate for the ability of your group), place two large baskets or bin liners of inflated balloons on the ground. Make sure you over-inflate the balloons to make popping easier!

4. At the starting signal, the first two contestants in each team run to their basket and grab a balloon. They then sit on it until it pops! As soon as it has popped, they run back to their team and tag the next player in line.

5. The first team to pop all their balloons wins.

Variations/advice:

▶ If you want to avoid the popping/banging frenzy, call the game 'Balloon shop', and instead, each child must collect a balloon and bring it back to their team's basket or bin liner.

Balloon points relay

This relay combines high-energy fun with counting practice.

Group size:

5+ players per team

Equipment:

▶ Small pieces of paper and a pen

▶ Balloons (enough for 2-4 per child)

How to play:

1. Mark some of the pieces of paper with point scores – 5, 10, 15, etc. – and don't forget to include 0 on some pieces. Roll the pieces of paper tightly and then push each one down the neck of a balloon, and blow the balloons up. All of this should be done before the game begins!

2. Gather the children together and sort them into two lines. Place the balloons in a cluster a short way away. When you give the signal, the two children at the head of each team rush forward to each pop a balloon and see if the paper inside it awards them points. No teeth or sharp objects allowed!

3. Once the balloon is popped, the player collects the piece of paper, puts it on a pile to one side (or hands it to a practitioner, if you have two colleagues available!) and returns to the back of their team line to wait for another turn.

4. Once all the balloons are popped, count up the points for each team; the team with the highest score wins.

Variations/advice:

▶ Watch carefully to make sure all the children are happy. Some don't like the sound of balloons popping and can get upset. That goes for adults as well as kids!

Catch the dragon's tail

The more children the merrier when playing this traditional Chinese game.

Group size:

10+

Equipment:

▶ Sashes or bibs (two different colours)

How to play:

1. The children form a line with their hands on the shoulders of the child in front.

2. The first five in line are the dragon's head and wear one colour sash or bib, and the last five in line are the dragon's tail and wear the other colour.

3. The players who are the dragon's head try to catch the tail by manoeuvring the line around so that they can tag the last player in the tail.

4. All the players in the tail do their best to hinder the dragon's head, but the line must not break!

Variations/advice:

▶ When the head catches the tail, the final tail player takes the first tail position and the first head player takes the last head position. All the other players move back one position. As mentioned before, it is also important that the head team and the tail team get the chance to be both the dodgers and the chasers.

Sharks and fish

Children will love this exciting running game, which works well as a warm-up exercise.

Group size:

5+ players per team

Equipment:

▶ None needed – just a space large enough for the children to 'swim' around in and an area marked 'Home'

How to play:

1. Choose a method of dividing the group up into two teams of equal numbers (see page 6): one team will be Sharks and the other will be Fish.

2. The Fish 'swim' around the room – arms by their sides and flapping their hands like gills/fins. The Sharks wait by the side.

3. On your signal – a shout of 'Shark!', or a whistle – one Shark enters the 'sea' and tries to catch the Fish. The Sharks move with their arms out in front of them, opening and closing them like big jaws.

4. Sharks catch Fish by touching them on the back – this is contact that must be taught carefully. A caught Fish moves to the side and becomes a Shark in the next round.

Variations/advice:

▶ If a lone Shark is struggling to catch any Fish or is doing so a little too slowly, call for another and another until the game seems to be progressing well. Don't forget to ensure that the Sharks get the chance to be Fish and vice versa.

Rock, paper, scissors — with legs!

A fun take on a traditional game.

Group size:

10+

Equipment:

▶ None needed

How to play:

1. Split the children into two teams.

2. The teams stand facing each other and, after a count of three, have the option of choosing from three different stances: rock = crouching down, paper = legs together, scissors = legs apart.

3. The teams should jump into the air and take up their chosen stance as they land. The usual rules apply: paper 'wraps' rock and wins; scissors 'cut' paper and win, rock 'blunts' scissors and wins. Decide on a winning points tally.

Variations/advice:

▶ A creative variation of this is called 'Giants, Dwarves and Wizards'. The teams line up as above but have the choice of being giants (standing up as tall as possible with arms above heads), dwarves (crouching down as small as possible while wriggling fingers out in front of them) or wizards (standing side-on while waving an imaginary wand). Giants 'crush' dwarves; dwarves 'tickle' wizards and make them drop their wands; wizards 'enchant' giants!

Coming in to land

Children are likely to develop their co-operation, co-ordination and trust in others in this team game.

Group size:

10+

Equipment:

▶ Material for blindfolds or soft hats that can be pulled down over the eyes

▶ Space big enough to be your runway!

How to play:

1. Divide the children into two teams; the teams take it in turns to be the 'plane' and the 'obstacles'.

2. One player in the plane team becomes the plane itself, and has his or her eyes covered (they can look down if this is easier), and the rest of the team verbally guide the blindfolded child around the obstacles, who are standing dotted along the runway.

3. The plane gets a penalty point for every obstacle it touches. If they get five points or more, the plane crashes and it the other team get the chance to be planes.

4. The game continues until everyone has had a chance to be the plane.

Variations/advice:

▶ You could have just one member of the team guiding the plane if it gets too noisy! You could also replace the human obstacles with things like chairs or books if you want to focus on concentration and quiet.

Letters and numbers

This activity is a great way of developing children's sense of shape and space.

Group size:

10+

Equipment:

▶ Sashes or bibs of two different colours to make two teams

How to play:

1. Tell the teams that you are going to call out a letter of the alphabet or a number. In their teams, the children should then work together to make that letter or number using their bodies. You decide on how long they have to achieve this and judge on the accuracy of their creations.

Variations/advice:

▶ Vary the number of children in a team. You could also challenge the children by stipulating upper case or lower case, and numbers up to 20 (or beyond)!

Round and back

This is a game that can be very easily adapted to add fresh challenges as the children become more experienced in playing it.

Group size:

6-10 players

Equipment:

► A beanbag for each team

► A marker/cone for each team

How to play:

1. Two teams line up one behind the other.

2. On your signal, the first player in each team runs, hops, walks or strides (or any other method of travel that you can think of!) up the course to a marker, carrying the beanbag in their hand (or balancing it on their head, to increase the level of difficulty). They go round the marker, make their way back to their team line and hand the beanbag over to next player.

3. Repeat this until everyone in the team has had a go. The team to finish first is the winner.

Variations/advice:
▶ There are many variants to this game. You could introduce obstacles or jumps to make it more difficult – it really is up to you!

Catch the stick

A plastic hoop can also be used in this simple game of quick reactions.

Group size:

Any

Equipment:

▶ A broomstick handle (or a PE hoop)

How to play:

1. Form a circle, facing inwards.

2. A practitioner stands in the centre of the circle holding a short broomstick upright on the ground by resting the palm of their hand on the top of it. They then suddenly remove their hand from the stick, calling a team by shouting out the colour of bib or sash.

3. A player from that team must try to catch the stick before it falls to the ground. If they succeed then their team scores points – you decide on how many – and the game is repeated.

Variations/advice:

▶ If you're nervous about using a broomstick, a PE hoop set spinning in the middle of the circle can be just as much fun and visually appealing. You can make the game more challenging by calling both colours at the same time or by calling a number of players from each team.

Hoop race

Racing directly parallel to the opposite team will encourage team spirit in this game of speed and dexterity!

Group size:

Any (but an equal number, to make two teams)

Equipment:

▶ Up to five small hoops (or skittles)

▶ Chalk or stickers as marks to place each hoop or skittle on

▶ Two larger hoops or mats

▶ A space large enough for running in

How to play:

1. The two teams line up in single file with a large hoop or mat in front of each team. Ahead of the large hoops, and about a yard apart, are two rows of smaller hoops (or skittles) on marks, extending in the direction in which the children are facing.

2. The first player in each team runs out and brings in the hoops/skittles one at a time, in any order they like, placing them in the large hoop (if using skittles, they must be placed upright). As soon as they have brought in all the hoops/skittles, the children run round and fall in at the back of their team line.

3. The second player then runs forward, and puts back the hoops/skittles back one by one on the marks. As soon as this is done they take their place at the back of the line. The third player repeats the actions of the first, bringing in the hoops/skittles. This is continued until all the players have been out and moved the equipment. The team with the first player once more at the front wins.

Variations/advice:

▶ You can adapt this as appropriate for your group. It may be that five pieces of equipment is too much or the skittles may be too heavy or ungainly. I have used small rubber quoits before and this has been successful as the children have been able to wear them up their arms like bangles!

Over and under

This is an extension of the activity 'Beanbag rush' on page 42.

Group size:

Any (but an equal number, to make two teams)

Equipment:

▶ Two beanbags or soft play objects

How to play:

1. The children are divided into two teams and stand in two lines. A soft, light object such as a beanbag is placed in the hands of the player at the front of each line.

2. At a given signal, each of these two players holds their beanbag above their head. It is seized by the player standing behind them who does the same, with player no. 3 then seizing it and passing it back over their shoulder to no. 4, and so on, right down the line. If the beanbag fails to pass through the hands of one of the players, you blow a whistle and the other team scores a point. The race starts again.

3. As the bag reaches the last player in the line, they cry 'about turn' and turning themselves, they then pass the bag between their legs to get it back to the start. The player immediately behind them catches hold of it and passes it on, between their legs, and so on down the line. The team in which no. 1 first gets hold of the bag, and holds it up above their head, wins.

Variations/advice:

▶ The beanbag must not be thrown down the line between the feet of the players, but must be passed from hand to hand, otherwise you must blow the whistle and the game begins again. A variation is for the children to stand straddle-legged, passing the beanbag backwards through the legs, and as soon as the last player in the line gets it they run up and take their place at the front, passing down the beanbag as before. This is repeated until all children have moved up to the front. The team in which player no.1 is first to reach the head of the line again wins.

Pass it on

Players need to be quick and careful in this race against the opposition.

Group size:

Any (but an equal number, to make two teams)

Equipment:

▶ Two tables/chairs

▶ A number of objects, varying in size from large to small

I will need

How to play:

1. The children are divided into two teams. They stand in lines facing each other, five paces apart. A chair or small table is placed at either end of each line. On the chairs at one end are a number of different-sized objects; for instance, a beanbag, a book, a button, a sheet of notepaper, a postage stamp, etc.

2. At the given signal, the player at the end of the line by the objects seizes one and passes it to their neighbour, who passes it on, and so on down the line. The last player puts the object on the empty table/chair next to them, and shouts 'down!' as they do so. As soon as they hear 'down!', the first player grabs another object and passes it on.

3. The team that has all the objects on the table/chair at the other end of the line first wins.

Variations/advice:

▶ Another way of playing this game, which should not be attempted until the above has been well practised, is to allow the objects to be passed down one after the other without waiting for the word 'down!'. This should make the players more careful about not dropping an object, as, if one does so, they find all the other objects are being piled up on them before they are ready to receive them. Objects must pass from hand to hand: if not, signal/whistle and award the opposite team one point.

Kangaroos

This traditional game, also known as 'Ladders', is bound to be a firm favourite.

Group size:

Any (but an equal number, to make two teams)

Equipment:

▶ Two tables/chairs

▶ None

How to play:

1. In a large space, the teams sit on the ground in two lines facing each other, with their legs close together and stretched forward, and their feet touching the feet of the player opposite. Each child should be about a yard away from those on their left and those on their right.

2. At the signal, the two players at the end of the two lines jump up, place hands on hips and hop, with both feet together, over the legs of all the players. As soon as they get to the end, each player runs back around the outside of their team line and sits back down in their place.

3. Next, the two children who are second in the line get up and do the same, hopping back over the children's legs to get to their places. No. 3 pair goes next, and so on, until the last players in the line have run up around the outside of the teams, and hopped over all the legs back to their places.

4. The team whose final player is the first to sit back down (and therefore complete the game) wins.

Variations/advice:

▶ You might want to make the spaces between the players wider and assess whether the children in your group possess the ability to clear the legs of their fellow players without making contact! Always err on the side of caution and adapt the rules accordingly.

Flag

This game requires time and practise, but once mastered it will cause much excitement! It could even be adapted as a dance to music.

Size of group:

6+

Equipment:

▶ Two small flags or squares of material

How to play:

1. Sort the children into teams of six. In each team, three of the children stand in single file at one end of the space and the other three stand exactly opposite them, three or more yards apart. The player at one end of one of the lines holds a small flag or square of material.

2. At the word 'Go!', the player holding the flag races to the player in the other half of their team who is standing immediately opposite them, and gives them the flag. This second player then races across and hands the flags to no. 2 in the line opposite, who races back and passes the flag to the player opposite him, and so on.

3. Each time a player hands the flag to the next player in the opposite team, they then run around the outside of that line and file in at the end. Therefore no.1 in line A passes the flag to no.1 in line B, then runs behind the line to become no. 4 in line B; meanwhile, no.1 in line B is carrying the flag across to no.2 in line A, then will run down the outside of line A and filter in at the end.

4. The winning team is the one in which the flag is quickest to return to the child who began the game with it.

Variations/advice:

▶ This game is fun but can be challenging! You have to be fully focussed on the way in which the players are participating and help those who are struggling or are having trouble with the rules.